Gems Of Wisdom

A Lifetime of Gathered Sayings to Inspire and Amuse

By
Marianne Bunge

(Posthumous)

With Photograph Credits to
Jennifer Beach

Copyrights © 2025

All Rights Reserved

No part of this book may be reproduced or transmitted in any form or by any means, electronic or mechanical, including photocopying, recording, or by any information storage and retrieval system without the written permission of the author, except where permitted by law.

All photographs courtesy of Jennifer Beach

All photographs by Jennifer Beach, with the exception of the photograph of Jennifer Beach, which was done professionally.

PREFACE

"The greatest test of courage is to bear defeat without losing heart."

~ Author unknown

This note was found in the book of collected sayings that follow. Whether the sayings contained herein are a collection of tidbits heard over her lifetime or some that the author drafted herself is unknown. These sayings were found in the author's own handwriting. For the purpose of this book, all sayings are attributed to authors unknown, and therefore, the book is a collection and no claim is made as an original work other than the photographs.

1

If there is such a thing as a good marriage, it's because it resembles friendship rather than love.

To appreciate the positive, one must accept the negative.

To be successful, the first thing to do is fall in love with your work.

Keep on going, and chances are that you will stumble on something, perhaps when you are least expecting it.

I have never heard of anyone stumbling on something sitting down.

It's one thing to know the path that lies before you. It's another thing to walk that path.

Anticipating pleasure is also a pleasure.

It's nice to see relatives get along, and the sooner some of them get along, the better.

A day away from some people is like a month in the country.

The chief difference between intelligence and stupidity is that intelligence has its limits.

The most powerful weapon is knowing what to do with the power you have.

In order to accomplish anything, you must first begin.

Dare to be what you are and to believe in your own individuality.

Most accidents are caused by motorists when their cars are in high gear and their minds are in neutral.

Personality is to man what perfume is to flower.

You are only young once, but you can stay immature almost indefinitely.

Be sure you are right, then go ahead.

If you lean over backwards, to be fair, it's harder for your enemies to knife you in the back.

We hate to have some people give us advice because we know how badly they need it themselves.

Parents can tell but never teach until they practice what they preach.

There are two sides to every conversation, and, in most cases, that's just from one individual.

Someone who cannot face up to a challenge is a coward, and one who doesn't live up to his word is a liar.

The one who listens is the one who understands.

There's no point in carrying the ball unless you know where the goal is.

Choice, not chance, determines destiny.

Success is a journey, not a destination.

The only difference between stumbling blocks and stepping stones is the way you use them.

No wise person ever wished to be younger.

Never gamble in heavy traffic—the cars may be stacked against you.

Bees are not as busy as we think they are—they just can't buzz any slower.

Only fools test the depth of the water with both feet.

When you fail to plan, you plan to fail.

Things forbidden have a secret charm.

Life does not have to be perfect to be wonderful.

The mind is like the stomach. It is not how much you put into it that counts, but how much it digests.

Even when a marriage is made in Heaven, the maintenance work has to be done here on Earth.

The mind, once stretched by a great idea, can never return to its original dimensions.

Horse sense is stable thinking coupled with the ability to say nay.

Build momentum by accumulating small successes.

Kindness is a language that the deaf can hear and the blind can see.

Do not let what you cannot do interfere with what you can do.

A closed mouth gathers no feet.

Choose a job you love and you will never have to work a day in your life.

We cannot direct the wind, but we can adjust the sails.

The people who think they are full of knowledge are especially annoying to those of us who are.

Too often are we swayed by our own insecurities.

Trust in those who listen, not those who just wait for an opportunity to talk.

We can judge the heart of a person by their treatment of animals.

Relationships are meaningless if you don't have a sense of self.

Self-reliance is the only road to true freedom, and being one's own person is its ultimate reward.

Life is like an all-you-can-eat buffet. No matter how full your plate is, you can't take it with you when you go.

Parents who are afraid to put their foot down usually have children who step on their toes.

Arriving at one goal is the starting point for another.

There's a difference between reasons that sound good and good, sound reasons.

He who looks down at his neighbors is usually living on a bluff.

English is a funny language; a fat chance and a slim chance are the same thing.

A person who never makes a mistake must get tired of doing nothing.

Those who disrespect get no respect.

Medical insurance is often a lot like wearing a hospital gown—you're never covered as much as you think you are.

An idea is a funny little thing that won't work unless you do.

Don't let yesterday use up too much of today.

Hating people is like burning down your own house to get rid of a rat.

What we learn with pleasure, we never forget.

Children need love, especially when they do not deserve it.

Love forgets mistakes: nagging about them parts the best of friends.

Happiness lies in the joy of achievement and the thrill of creative effort.

Be humble, or you'll stumble.

The best way to ease your troubles is to help others in theirs.

A dog is a dog except when he is facing you; then he is Mr. Dog.

When it comes to plumbing, it is not always a good thing to have your cup run over.

The best thing learned from pets is to always greet loved ones with affection.

We are usually convinced more easily by reasons we have found ourselves than by those which have occurred to others.

Don't just entertain new ideas—put them to work.

Things are seldom what they seem.

There is never a time to quit and give up on yourself or those you love.

When you start to look like your passport picture, you know you need a vacation.

Since time flies, it's up to you to be the navigator.

Be kind but not foolish.

One of the most common mistakes is thinking your worries are over when your children get married.

10

A diamond is a chunk of coal that is made good under pressure.

It's nice to know that when you help someone up a hill, you're a little closer to the top yourself.

When you talk, you repeat what you already know; when you listen, you often learn something.

Motivation is what gets you going; habit is what keeps you going.

Our necessities are few, but our wants are endless.

One who graduates today and stops learning tomorrow is uneducated the day after.

I hear, and I forget. I see, and I remember. I do, and I understand.

The problem is that the key to success doesn't always fit your ignition.

11

Doing nothing is the most tiresome job in the world because you can't stop and rest.

Most people are about as happy as they make up their minds to be.

He who plans his program for tomorrow takes the confusion out of the day.

There's no free tuition in the school of experience.

Fear and faith cannot keep the house together; when one enters, the other departs.

Boredom is also known as a state of 'mine.'

Hot words never resulted in cool judgment.

The test of good manners is to be able to put up pleasantly with bad ones.

The door of wisdom swings on hinges of common sense and uncommon thoughts.

12

Budget: a mathematical confirmation of your suspicions.

In three words, I can sum up everything I've learned about life: It goes on.

If you can't win, make the fellow ahead of you break the record.

Nature, to be commanded, must be obeyed.

The fruit derived from labor is the sweetest of all pleasures.

He who is content can never be ruined.

Of all days, the day on which one has not laughed is surely the most wasted.

A gifted leader is one who is capable of touching your heart.

Unused experience is a dead loss.

If you don't want anyone to know it, don't do it.

He who angers you controls you.

13

When spider webs unite, they can tie up a lion.

Real friends are those who, when you've made a fool of yourself, don't feel that you've done a permanent job.

The way to get things done is not to mind who gets the credit for doing them.

An optimist may be wrong, but he bears mistakes with fortitude.

Some people are making such thorough plans for rainy days that they aren't enjoying today's sunshine.

When you're safe at home, you wish you were having an adventure; when you're having an adventure, you wish you were safe at home.

The chief ability of an executive should be their ability to recognize ability.

Keep your nose out of another's mess.

There is no power greater than restraint.

Contentment diminishes potential.

If you don't have a sense of humor, you probably don't have any sense at all.

14

If you want to kill any idea in the world today, get a committee working on it.

We make our future by the best use of the present.

Every great person learned how to obey, whom to obey, and when to disobey.

It takes an honest person to admit if they're tired or just lazy.

A comic is a person who originates classic jokes.

Friendship is like a bank account. You can't continue to draw on it without making deposits.

When man learned that he could not live on bread alone, he invented the sandwich.

One who says the days of opportunity are over is copping out.

15

You can never speak a kind word too soon, for you never know how soon it will be too late.

Throw a lucky man into the sea, and he will come up with a fish in his mouth.

Getting a new idea should be like sitting on a tack; it should make you get up and do something about it.

Money used to talk, then it whispered; now it just sneaks off.

To get maximum attention, it's hard to beat a big mistake.

Offering good advice may be noble and grand, but it's not the same as a helping hand.

Initiative is doing the right thing at the right time without having to be told.

He who walks in when others walk out is a true friend.

When a man and woman marry, they become one. The trouble starts when they try to decide which one.

16

It's better to have a backache from working in the garden than a headache from worrying about the rest of the earth.

One who begins too much accomplishes little.

One who aims at nothing is sure to hit it.

Mother asks Junior, after his first day at school, "Did you learn anything today?" "No," he says in disgust, "I have to go back tomorrow."

It's not hard to make a mountain out of a molehill; just add a little dirt.

It's what you learn after you know it all that counts.

A company is judged by the president it keeps. So is a country.

Regardless of circumstances, each person lives in a world of their own making.

17

A successful person is one who can lay a firm foundation with the bricks that others throw at them.

Everything is difficult at first.

A good deal of trouble has been caused in the world by too much intelligence and too little wisdom.

Life is just one fool thing after another; love is just two fool things after each other.

Last night, I read a book that brought tears to my eyes—my bankbook.

Maybe we can keep warm next year by burning our bills.

Experience is about the cheapest thing a person can get if they're smart enough to get it secondhand.

One of the hardest decisions to make in life is when to start middle age.

Slow and steady wins the race.

Being serious isn't all that important. What counts is knowing what to be serious about.

The time to teach respect for authority is in the playpen instead of the state pen.

18

Don't be afraid of opposition. Remember, a kite rises against, not with, the wind.

The only place where success comes before work is in the dictionary.

If you don't get everything you want, think of the things you don't get that you don't want.

You are only what you are when no one is looking.

A fair-weather friend is one who is always around when he needs you.

He who is overcautious will accomplish little in life.

In prosperity, our friends know us; in adversity, we know our friends.

If you're looking for a big opportunity, look for a big problem.

Find someone to encourage; it will lift you up too.

Never make a decision based on fear.

The best time to keep your shirt on is when you're hot under the collar!

19

We are inclined to believe those we do not know because they have never deceived us.

To do injustice is more disgraceful than to suffer it.

Once bitten, twice shy.

Be a dreamer; they make things happen.

There is no need to show your ability before everyone.

You can't build a reputation on what you are going to do.

Sign in a store clock display: "There's no present like the time."

To err is human, but to really foul things up requires a computer.

One who removes a mountain begins by carrying away small stones.

The truth is always the strongest argument.

Few things are more dangerous to a person's reputation than having nothing to do and plenty of time in which to do it.

20

A successful marriage is one in which you fall in love many times, always with the same person.

He who is carried away by his own importance seldom has far to walk back.

The love that you give becomes the love that you get.

People on ego trips should do others a favor and buy one-way tickets.

Real generosity is doing something nice for someone who will never find it out.

Always keep your head up, but be careful to keep your nose at a friendly level.

Self-control is a virtue you never knew you had until you argue with the boss.

To understand is to forgive.

The past is valuable to you as a guidepost but dangerous if used as a hitching post.

21

The trouble with being a parent is that by the time we're experienced, we're unemployed.

To make your dreams come true, you have to stay awake.

Even a fish wouldn't get in trouble if it kept its mouth shut.

Don't be afraid to go out on a limb, that's where the fruit is.

A person with a reservoir of knowledge is not well educated unless they know when to turn the spigot off and on.

To satisfy the itch for money, stretch for it.

If a friend is in trouble, don't annoy him by asking if there is anything you can do. Think up something appropriate and do it.

One who rolls up their sleeves seldom loses their shirt.

22

He who speaks much is much mistaken.

There is no vulture-like despair.

If you could kick the person responsible for most of your problems, you wouldn't be able to sit down for a month.

Conscience is an inner voice that warns us someone is watching.

Many people are not failures. They just started at the bottom and are stuck there.

To speak kindly does not hurt the tongue. Money will buy a fine dog, but only kindness will make him wag his tail.

A critic is a wet blanket that soaks everything it touches.

If a cluttered desk is an indication of a cluttered mind, what is indicated by an empty desk?

Vision is the art of seeing things invisible.

Bores are people who bring happiness whenever they go.

23

The surest way to be deceived is to think oneself more clever than others.

An opportunist pulls himself up by your bootstraps.

Take time to play—it is the secret of youth.

Originality is simply a pair of fresh eyes.

Good judgment comes from experience; experience comes from bad judgment.

When an adolescent gets some money, the first thing he wants is a car; the next thing he wants is some money.

The wheel was man's greatest invention until he got behind it.

Speaking of money, it doesn't make you completely happy, but it sure quiets the nerves.

There are usually two sides to every argument, but no end.

They who do not show their love do not love.

First think, then speak. Put your mind in gear before opening your mouth.

A little spark kindles a great fire.

One way to get ahead and stay ahead is to use your head.

If there's a job to be done, select a busy person; the other kind has no time.

If you don't know where you're going, you'll wind up somewhere else.

Coaches who can outline plays on a blackboard are a dime a dozen. The ones who win get inside their players' heads and motivate them.

The fool wanders—the wise man travels.

A dollar goes a long way today. You can carry it around for weeks before you find something you can buy with it.

When fighting with monsters, be careful that you yourself do not become one.

25

Liberty is not the right to do as we please but the opportunity to do what is right.

Not everything that is faced can be changed, but nothing can be changed until it is faced.

The greatest things that one can have are a free spirit and an open mind.

The guy riding a high horse is heading for a fall.

Live simply but think deeply.

Our destiny changes with our thoughts; we shall become what we wish to become and do what we wish to do when our habitual thoughts correspond with our desires.

The worst bankrupt in the world is a person who has lost their enthusiasm. Let them lose everything but enthusiasm, and they will come through again to success.

26

The mind is like television: when it goes blank, it's a good idea to turn off the sound.

Laughter is the brush that sweeps away the cobwebs of the heart.

Falling down doesn't make you a failure, but staying down does.

The art of being wise is the art of knowing what to overlook.

Before you drink at a brook, it's best to know its source.

Grief can take care of itself, but to get the full value of joy, you must have someone to share it with.

Believers eventually become achievers.

There is no use whatsoever trying to help people who do not help themselves.

The person who is tactful has the knack of making a point without making an enemy.

You are your greatest possession.

The true art of memory is the art of attention.

If you don't scale the mountain, you can't view the plain.

Beware of a silent dog and still water.

Too often do we point the finger at others when something goes wrong, when in reality, we should be looking at ourselves.

You can take better care of your secret than another can.

Where there is an open mind, there will always be a frontier.

Common sense is not so common.

If each one sweeps before their own door, the whole street is clean.

It is easier to stay out than to get out.

Chatter is a form of conversation where much is spoken and little is said.

Strive for excellence, not perfection.

Criticism never built a house, wrote a play, composed a song, painted a picture, or improved a marriage.

A problem well-stated is a problem half-solved.

Those who want little always have enough.

Be alert for opportunities to show praise and appreciation.

Words in haste do friendships waste.

The secret to getting ahead is getting started.

All people smile in the same language.

Make your enemy your friend.

Life can be pretty grim when you pass eighty, especially if there's a state trooper behind you.

When your work speaks well for you, don't interrupt.

29

The beautiful is not always expensive, and the expensive is not always beautiful.

Friends may come and go, but enemies accumulate.

You all have powers you never dreamed of.

Happy is the house that shelters a friend.

Where there is room in the heart, there is always room in the house.

Most of the excitement of life is hunting for some.

We can only appreciate the miracle of a sunrise if we have waited in darkness.

The world should make peace first and then make it last.

It never occurs to some people that there's a big difference between giving advice and lending a hand.

An acquaintance that begins with a compliment is sure to develop into a real friendship.

Don't look for happiness—create it.

Words are things, and a small drop of ink, falling like dew upon a thought, produces that which makes thousands, perhaps millions, think.

Good things are not done in a hurry.

A person enters a casino to get something for nothing and exits when he gets nothing for something.

Always drive as if your family were in the other car.

Live so your friends can defend you—but never have to.

If you can laugh at it, you can live with it.

Only those who will risk going too far can possibly find out how far one can go.

Think for yourself, and nobody can outsmart you.

Values are not trendy items that are casually traded in.

31

The minute you settle for less than you deserve, you get even less than you settled for.

Contentment is the smother of invention.

You are a king by your own fireside, as much as any monarch on his throne.

It's the little things that matter the most: what good is a bathtub without a plug?

It's what you learn after you know it all that counts.

You collect things; they collect dust.

Charm is a glow within a person that casts a most becoming light on others.

Not to know is bad, not to strive to know is worse.

It is an act of arrogance for someone to decide what is best for someone else.

The tongue has no bone, yet it crushes.

32

Take a lesson from tea—its real strength comes out when it gets into hot water.

An honest person tells the truth; a tactless person tells the truth bluntly.

Some people count time; others make the time count.

Blood is thicker than water, and it boils quicker too.

The time you need your temper the most is after you lose it.

You must be the change you wish to see in the world.

A mistake proves that at least someone tried.

Now I don't know what will happen to me; my fortune cookie contradicted my horoscope.

People are too quick to judge the unique and accept the norm.

The fortunate are less likely to be charitable than those who have nothing to give.

33

The bamboo that bends is stronger than the oak that resists.

The harder you work, the luckier you get.

It is no great thing to be humble when you are brought low, but to be humble when you are praised is a great and rare attainment.

The businessman who is not afraid to adventure is the one most likely to succeed.

Some modern artists fling paint at a canvas, wipe their brushes off with a rag, and then exhibit the rag.

There is no difference between mind and matter— the mind is matter, gray matter.

The only time a fisherman tells the truth is when he calls another fisherman a liar.

Feed your belief, and your doubts will starve to death.

People will doubt what you say, but they'll always believe what you do. Actions speak louder than words.

A small house will hold as much happiness as a large one.

He who laughs, lasts.

Talk is cheap—do something.

Even a mosquito doesn't get a pat on the back until she starts to work.

Whether you're on the road or in an argument, when you see red, it's time to stop.

A smile is the light in the window of a face which shows that the heart is at home.

Everyone thinks of changing the world, but no one thinks of changing themselves.

A bore is someone who tells you his life story from A to Zzzzz.

The best thing you can give someone is a chance.

Speak well of your enemies; you made them.

It's alright to be cautious—but even a turtle never gets anywhere until he sticks his head out.

The person who raises roses in his garden also does kindness to his neighbors.

True teaching is not that which gives knowledge but that which stimulates pupils to gain it.

We are only truly lost when we give up hope.

In the middle of difficulty lies opportunity.

Procrastination is opportunity's natural assassin.

By the time you acquire a nest egg, inflation has turned it into chicken feed.

When we were kids, ten cents was big money. How dimes have changed!

Confidence is the feeling you have before you fully understand the situation.

Cherish your visions and your dreams as they are the children of your soul, the blueprints of your ultimate achievements.

For the resolute and determined, there is time and opportunity.

A miser is a person who lives within his income—he's also called a magician.

To teach is to learn twice.

It is never wise to argue with a fool; the bystander doesn't know which is which.

Some carve out the future while others just whittle away the time.

When I hear somebody sigh that "Life is hard," I am always tempted to ask, "Compared to what?"

A lawyer is a person who profits from your experience.

The best tranquilizer is a good conscience.

The person who knows it all has a lot to learn.

Adopt the pace of nature, her secret is patience.

He who considers too much will perform little.

Marrying for money is the hardest way to earn it.

The best way to avoid a nosebleed is to keep out of other people's business.

One thing the future can guarantee is that anything can happen.

Happiness is like potato salad when shared with others: it's a picnic.

The hardest thing to give is in.

Opportunity knocks only once; temptation leans on the doorbell.

Wit is the spice of conversation.

Humor is a lifeboat we use on life's river.

Life without hope is a life without meaning.

Time doesn't heal, but it makes the hurt bearable.

You only live once, and if you work at night, once is enough.

A budget is a sort of conscience that doesn't keep you from spending but makes you feel guilty about it.

Love your enemies—it will drive them crazy.

Too bad you can't invest in taxes; they are the only thing sure to go up.

Do not mistake activity for achievement.

There are no shortcuts to any place worth going.

If time was irrelevant, would we still keep track of it?

The recipe for a good speech includes some shortening.

People have minds like blotters; they soak up everything but get it all backward.

The will to live supersedes everything inflicted on the mind and body.

Wrinkles should merely indicate where smiles have been.

Cooperation is spilled with 2 letters—we.

No legacy is as rich as honesty.

Honesty is the first chapter in the book of wisdom.

One thing you can learn by watching the clock is that it passes the time by keeping its hands busy.

You cannot push anyone up a ladder unless he is willing to climb it himself.

Opportunity is missed by most people because it is dressed in overalls and looks like work.

A wise man controls his temper. He knows anger causes mistakes.

Learning is to the mind what exercise is to the body.

All our dreams can come true if we have the courage to pursue them.

Factory sign: IF YOU HAVE NOTHING TO DO, PLEASE DON'T DO IT HERE.

Cooperation will solve many problems. Even freckles would be a nice tan if they got together.

The bee that makes the honey doesn't hang around the hive.

Life is a grindstone. But whether it grinds us down or polishes us up depends on what we're made of.

41

The indispensable first step to getting the things you want out of life is this: DECIDE WHAT YOU WANT.

Never try to teach a pig to sing. It wastes your time and annoys the pig.

Laugh at yourself first before anyone else can.

In every insurance policy, the big print giveth and the small print taketh away.

We never know the worth of water till the well is dry.

In the good old days, they also used to speak of the good old days.

He who moves not forward goes backward.

Have character—don't be one.

After you've heard two eyewitness accounts of an auto accident, you begin to worry about history.

The reason things go in one ear and out the other is that there's nothing to block the traffic.

It's hard to raise a family nowadays, especially in the morning.

The only reason some people are lost in thought is that they are total strangers there.

Anybody can face a crisis—it's this day-to-day living that wears us out.

An optimist builds castles in the sky, a dreamer lives there, and a realist collects rent from both of them.

The only food that doesn't go up in price is food for thought.

We are only truly lost when we give up hope.

It is better to deserve honors and not have them than to have them and not deserve them.

For the resolute and determined, there is time and opportunity.

Great boasters—little doers.

To hate, fatigues.

Success is getting what you want. Happiness is wanting what you get.

Anger cannot be dishonest.

If I had to sum up in one word what makes a good manager, I'd say decisiveness.

The buck stopped before it got here.

No one can be caught in places they do not visit.

Self-expression is good; self-control is better.

Character doesn't change: the little crybaby eventually becomes a groan adult.

Ideas are like children: there are none so wonderful as your own.

Let us keep our mouths shut and our pens dry until we know the facts.

Hindsight is the ability to see an opportunity, but only after you've missed it.

The right to be heard does not automatically include the right to be taken seriously.

Soft words are hard arguments.

History teaches us the mistakes that we are going to make.

One who has lost confidence can lose nothing more.

Fear usually comes as a result of ignorance.

A friend is a gift you give yourself.

The bare truth in the newspaper does not always get the proper coverage.

Good humor makes all things tolerable.

Let us not get tired of doing what's right—for after a while, we will reap a harvest of blessings if we don't get discouraged and we don't give up.

As I grow to understand life less and less, I learn to love it more and more.

Learn to show cheerfulness, even when you don't feel like it.

It takes both rain and sunshine to make a rainbow.

Opportunities are seldom labeled.

Love does not weigh rights and privileges too carefully because it prompts each other to bear the burden of the other.

I don't like to repeat gossip but what else can you do with it?

The best way to save face is to keep the lower half shut.

Strange how much you've got to know before you know how little you know.

A fool dreams of wealth, a wise man of happiness.

All of us could take a lesson from the weather—it pays no attention to criticism.

The best way to get a bad law repealed is to enforce it strictly.

All the treasures of Earth cannot bring back one lost moment.

Little said is the soonest mended.

Did you hear about the fellow who climbed the ladder of success wrong by wrong?

Man is the only animal that hasn't an international language.

Responsibility is the thing people dread most of all. Yet, it is the only thing in the world that develops us.

The best of humor is the kind that enables you to see at once what isn't safe to laugh at.

Nothing makes a scandal grow more like a grain of truth.

Don't judge your progress by comparing yourself to someone else.

The power of a kind word or deed is indescribable.

Don't be concerned with who's right, but what's right.

Winners do what others don't want to do.

Character is like the foundation of a house—it is below the surface.

When you're dying of thirst, it's too late to think about digging a well.

Envy is a kind of praise.

Learn from others' mistakes; you can't make them all.

A shirker is a person who, to say the least, is always ready to do the least.

We should live and learn, but by the time we learn, it's too late to live.

The chief advantage of having money is that you don't have to worry about not having it.

Minutes at the table don't put on the weight—it's the seconds.

By the time you get your shoulder to the wheel, your nose to the grindstone, and your ear to the ground, it's time for lunch.

Leave everything a little better than you found it.

Always tell the truth; it's the easiest thing to remember.

Not keeping an appointment is an act of clear dishonesty. You may as well borrow a person's money as their time.

History repeats itself, and that's one of the things that's wrong with history.

Education is what you get from reading the small print in a contract.

Conversation is an exercise of the mind. Gossiping is merely an exercise of the tongue.

Money, if it does not bring you happiness, will at least help you to be miserable in comfort.

People generally do not appreciate what they do not suffer for.

The lazier a man is today, the more he has to do tomorrow.

Fools think they need no advice, but the wise listen to others.

Wise men change their minds; fools never.

Next to good judgment, diamonds and pearls are the rarest things in the world.

Money talks—it says goodbye.

All of us would gladly accept the advice of our moral superiors; the difficulty is finding any.

Obstacles are those frightful things you see when you take your eyes off your goal.

Those who say you can't take it with you never saw a car packed for vacation.

51

Life is not measured by the number of breaths we take but by the moments that take our breath away.

What a terrible time people have trying to have a good time.

Many people wait for their ship to come in even though they never sent one out.

Strange thing how trouble acts differently on folks: it's like hot weather—sours the milk but sweetens the apples.

One that will cheat at play will cheat you anyway.

Next year, 4 million kids will turn sixteen and 8 million parents will turn pale.

As we acquire more knowledge, things do not become more comprehensible but more mysterious.

The trouble with the world is that laziness is seldom curable and never fatal.

Don't refuse to accept criticism; get all the help you can.

We learn and grow and are transformed not so much by what we do but why and how we do it.

If we stopped to think more, we would stop to think more.

Never, never, never, never give up.

The most dangerous of all falsehoods is a slightly distorted truth.

People who give their children habits of industry provide for them better than by giving them a fortune.

A good leader inspires people to have confidence in him. A great leader inspires people to have confidence in themselves.

Drive sensibly and responsibly. If you don't, your present car may last you a lifetime.

Trouble is only opportunity in work clothes.

I regret often that I have spoken, seldom when I have been silent.

He who wrestles with us strengthens our nerves and sharpens our skills. Our antagonist is our helper.

All marriages are happy. It's the living together afterward that causes all the trouble.

The word impossible is peculiar because if you examine it, most of it is possible.

Experience is what you've got when you're too old to get a job.

If a link is broken, the whole chain breaks.

We don't need more strength or more ability or greater opportunity. What we need is to use what we have.

Reading is to the mind what exercise is to the body.

Scars are a definition of life.

The biggest fool of all is the person who refuses to profit from his mistakes.

A new name for laziness is voluntary inertia.

All roads to success and achievement are uphill.

What's done to children, they will do to society.

He who would govern others, first should be the master of himself.

It isn't the mountains that trip people up but the molehills.

55

Whoever gossips to you will gossip about you.

The world needs more warm hearts and fewer hot heads.

Failure is the path of least resistance.

After all is said and done, more is said than done.

One who cannot obey cannot command.

You can't measure the whole world with your own yardstick.

When happiness gets into your system, it's bound to break out on your face.

In an argument, the best weapon to hold is your tongue.

The secret of happy living is not to do what you like but to like what you do.

It is never too late to mend.

Justice is truth in action.

One who makes a mistake and doesn't correct it is making another mistake.

Everything comes to him who hustles while he waits.

There is never jealousy where there is not strong regard.

Every path hath a puddle.

Never answer a question until it is asked.

There are many essential oils in the industry, but the best one is still elbow grease.

Little drops of water, little grains of sand, make the mighty ocean and the pleasant land.

A clean conscience is a soft pillow.

Providence sends food for the birds but does not throw it in the nest.

He who is waiting for something to turn up might start with his own shirtsleeves.

No matter how well you nurse a grudge, it will never get better.

Curiosity will conquer fear even more than bravery will.

Work joyfully and peacefully, knowing that the right thoughts and efforts will inevitably bring about the right results.

There are four steps to accomplishment:

Plan purposely

Prepare productively

Proceed positively

Pursue persistently

Progress is impossible without change.

Those who cannot change their mind cannot change anything.

If anything makes a child thirstier than going to bed, it's knowing his parents have gone to bed too.

Enthusiasm is the highest paid quality on earth.

The most important thing a father can do for his children is love their mother.

Paying attention to simple little things that most people neglect makes a few people rich.

How a person plays the game shows something of their character. How one loses shows all of it.

It is never too late to become who you might have been.

The line between self-confidence and conceit is very narrow.

The reason talk is cheap is that supply far outpaces demand.

An optimist is one who makes the best of it when he gets the worst of it.

If you are not generous with a meager income, you will not be generous with abundance.

Before pollution, people used to get airsick only on planes.

One good thing about apathy is you don't have to exert yourself to show you're sincere about it.

59

Make no little plans; they have no magic to stir one's blood. Make big plans, aim high, and work.

Don't marry for money; you can borrow it more cheaply.

When the head aches, the body is out of tune.

Worry is the interest paid on trouble before it falls due.

No member of a crew is praised for the rugged individuality of his rowing.

Disappointment should always be taken as a stimulant and never viewed as a discouragement.

What one cannot, another can.

A perfect summer day is when the sun is shining, the breeze is blowing, the birds are singing, and the lawn mower is broken.

The most important trip you may take in life is meeting people halfway.

Out of the spark shall spring the flame.

Vision is only a minute aspect of success.

A normal person knows right from wrong; a good person admits when they're wrong.

You fall the way you lean.

Just because you have the gift of sight doesn't mean you can see.

One of the worst things about retirement is that you have to drink coffee on your own time.

People always call it luck when you've acted more sensibly than they have.

It takes a lot of horse sense to maintain a stable life.

61

Preconceived notions are the locks on the door to wisdom.

Seven days without laughter make one weak.

There is nothing more frightful than ignorance at work.

Never judge a man's actions until you know his motives.

A man who gives in when he is wrong is wise.
A man who gives in when he is right is married.

There is no grief like the grief that does not speak.

Good advice is no better than poor advice unless you follow it.

Some people approach every problem with an open mouth.

He who wants to finish the race must stay on the track.

Age is a high price to pay for maturity.

Don't cross the bridge until you have the exact toll ready.

A gifted leader is one who is capable of touching your heart.

It is not the IQ but the I WILL that is important in education.

One of these days is none of these days.

The reason a dog is a man's best friend is because he does not pretend, he proves it.

You really believe in heredity when your child's report card is all As.

Common sense is the knack of seeing things as they are and doing things as they ought to be done.

Only the brave know how to forgive.

Work is love made visible.

A problem is a chance for you to do your best.

Better to lose the anchor than the whole ship.

Tact is the ability to arrive at conclusions without expressing them.

Empty barrels make the most noise.

You can judge a man by his enemies as well as by his friends.

The trouble with the world is not that people know too little, but that they know so many things that ain't so.

Luck is what happens when preparation meets opportunity.

Kindness affects more than severity.

A good laugh is sunshine in a house.

Not every question deserves an answer.

Some people remind us of blisters, they don't show until the work is done.

Don't be afraid to take a big step if it's required. You can't cross a chasm in two small jumps.

Conversation enriches understanding, but solitude is the school of genius.

A gossip always gets caught in its own mouth trap.

Gossip is nothing more than mouth-to-mouth recitation.

Some are wise, and some are otherwise.

If you don't learn from your mistakes, there's no sense in making them.

Do not handicap your children by making their lives easy.

A small tear relieves a great sorrow.

You can tell when you're on the right road—it's uphill.

The happiest people are those who are too busy to notice.

The train of failure usually runs on the track of laziness.

Beware of little expenses—a small leak will sink a ship.

Criticism wouldn't be so hard to take if it weren't sometimes right.

The golden rule in life is moderation in all things.

Fear of the future is a waste of the present.

Procrastination is the art of keeping up with yesterday.

If you can't heal the wound, don't tear it open.

You can always tell the smart-alecky; he takes every opportunity to show off his wide range of misinformation.

Don't pray for an easier life; pray to be a stronger person.

Time is nature's way of keeping everything from happening at once.

The first law of ecology is that everything is related to everything else.

Home can be a state of mind.

The disadvantage of being a person others can depend on is that others too often do.

A weeding job, once completed, must soon thereafter be repeated.

Cleverness is not wisdom.

If the idea you had three days ago still looks good, do it!

Just when you think you've got it in the bag, the bag breaks.

A little more drive, a little more pluck, a little more work, and that's luck.

Give a person a fish, and you feed them for a day; teach that person to use the Internet, and they won't bother you for weeks.

The reason that truth is stranger than fiction is that there is less of it.

Before you start to change things, at least take the time to find out why it is being done the way it is now.

Some of the finest dancers and musicians are members of the animal kingdom.

Hear what others say to you, but remain in tune with your own inner voices

A dragon does not always have to be slain; it can sometimes be befriended.

The less change there is in your life, the more stressful change will be.

Speak a little, say a lot.

Make the most of yourself, for that is all there is of you.

One learns with the eyes and ears, not the mouth.

One cannot touch without being touched.

What we didn't do yesterday causes most of the trouble today.

People with tact have less to retract.

Life is a test that has more questions than answers.

People who think they can run the earth should begin with a small garden.

The most important things in life aren't things.

Life is a work of art designed by the one who lives it.

Focus on your goal. Name the steps it will take you to achieve it.

The trouble with being punctual is that nobody's there to appreciate it.

Pride goeth before a fall, but it goes a lot quicker after one.

After silence, that which comes nearest to expressing the expressionless, is music.

There's nothing wrong with the younger generation that the older generation didn't outgrow.

Half the evil in the world is gossip started by good people.

Mountain climbers always rope themselves together, probably to prevent the sensible ones from going home.

If you want to enjoy your lawn more, think of your weeds as plants and your dandelions as flowers.

When love and skill work together, expect a masterpiece.

Years may wrinkle the skin, but to give up enthusiasm wrinkles the soul.

Shoot for the moon; even if you miss, you'll land among the stars.

The most effective of all highway safety signs is on the car marked 'Police.'

If it weren't for dogs, some people would never go for a walk.

Take a tip from nature: your ears weren't made to shut; your mouth was.

There is nothing so small that it can't be blown out of proportion.

When it is dark enough, you can see the stars.

An optimist is one who believes what's going to be will be postponed.

Be yourself. Who's better qualified?

You can have it all. You just can't have it all at once.

You can't stay mad at somebody who makes you laugh.

The biggest mistake you can make is to believe that you work for someone else.

Go confidently in the direction of your dreams. Live the life you've imagined.

Interesting people are people who are interested.

Occasional failure is the price of improvement.

The one thing worse than a quitter is the one who is afraid to begin.

The chief danger in life is that you may take too many precautions.

To win the race is to rise each time we fall.

You must do the things you think you cannot do.

People are paid not for what they know but for what they do with what they know.

It isn't what happens; it's how you deal with it.

The journey is the reward.

All gardening is landscape painting.

Never give up, for that is just the place and time the tide will turn.

Action springs not from thought but from a readiness for responsibility.

It is not what we take up but what we give up that makes us rich.

Every moment of resistance to temptation is a victory.

Good examples have twice the value of good advice.

On the other hand, you have different fingers.

In the long run, the pessimist may be proven right, but the optimist has a better time on the trip.

We don't stop playing because we grow old—we grow old because we stop playing.

Control yourself: remember that anger is only one letter short of danger.

To get the best out of an argument, stay out of it.

I can resist everything except temptation.

The doorstep to the temple of wisdom is the knowledge of our ignorance.

Observe yourself living.

Being overlooked can sometimes be a blessing.

To accomplish great things, one must not only act but dream.

When you're rundown, the best thing to take is the license number.

Beware of ambition; it can drive you into a lot of work.

Tact is the art of putting your foot down without stepping on anyone's toes.

If criticism had any real power, the skunk would have been extinct by now.

Trust only those who stand to lose as much as you when things go wrong.

You cannot get ahead while you are getting even.

Blessed are they who have nothing to say and cannot be persuaded to say it.

Generalizations are generally wrong.

The real reason opportunity is seldom recognized is that it usually comes disguised as hard work.

If you view a problem closely enough, you will recognize yourself as part of the problem.

One of the wonders of life is the wonder of life.

You are only young once; after that, you have to blame your mistakes on something else.

Frequently, the person with the least expertise has the most opinions.

74

We will never have universal peace until each nation is satisfied with the piece it has.

Spring comes unusually late or unusually early every year—as usual.

The journey is often more interesting than the destination.

The taxpayer—that's someone who works for the government but doesn't have to take a civil service exam.

How much would you be worth if you lost all your money?

There is no substitute for brains, but the next best thing is silence.

When opportunity knocks, some people wait for it to break the door down and come in.

A person never realizes how many friends he has until he buys a cottage on a lake.

People who complain they don't get all they deserve don't realize how lucky they are.

You can test a person's sense of humor by what he laughs at and his sense of values by what he doesn't laugh at.

Never argue with anyone; remember, he too has a right to his own opinion.

Freedom rings where opinions clash.

There is no one so tactless as the person who says what everyone is thinking.

Lazy people are much maligned: they are perfectly willing to work, provided it doesn't involve effort, exertion, labor, or toil.

One of the secrets of life is to make stepping stones out of stumbling blocks.

Never underestimate your power to change yourself.

Never give up on what you really want. The person with big dreams is more powerful than the one with all the facts.

Live your life so that your epitaph can read, "No Regrets."

It's never too late to learn, and it's never too early either.

When in doubt, go home.

A truth that's told with bad intent beats all the lies you can invent.

You always pass failure on the way to success.

Miser: one who is perfectly content to let the rest of the world go buy.

Where there's a will, there are dissatisfied relatives.

It's surprising how much hard work some people will put into resisting hard work.

Silence is the ultimate weapon of power.

Get-well cards have become so humorous that if you don't get sick, you're missing a lot of fun.

Two weeks is about the ideal length of time to retire.

77

To be happy at home is the ultimate aim of all ambition.

At no time is self-control more difficult than in times of success.

The easiest way to find something lost is to buy a replacement.

As a person grows wiser, they talk less and say more.

Do it tomorrow; you've made enough mistakes for one day.

Never argue with an addict. They drag you down to their level and then beat you with experience.

The world is full of willing people—some willing to work, the rest willing to let them.

If it is illegal to send obscene material through the mail; how come my electric bill gets through?

Do something! Either lead, follow, or get out of the way.

The egotist says, "Everyone has a right to my opinion."

About the time we learn to make the most of life, most of it is gone.

If 50 million people say a foolish thing, it is still a foolish thing?

An optimist is one who sends a package by parcel post and marks it 'Rush.'

There is a limit to everything except the number of untrue things people will believe.

Human beings have willpower; mules have won't power.

Small things do matter; more people are killed each year by the bite of mosquitoes than are stepped on by charging elephants.

A fine is a tax you pay for doing wrong, and a tax is a fine you pay for doing right.

By the time you have money to burn, the fire has gone out.

Everything comes to him who hustles
while he waits.

There is never jealousy where there
is not strong regard.

Every path hath a puddle.

Never answer a question
until it is asked.

There are many essential oils in
industry, but the best one is
still elbow grease.

Little drops of water, little grains of sand,
make the mighty ocean and the pleasant land.

A clean conscience is a soft pillow.

Providence sends food for the birds,
but does not throw it in the nest.

He who is waiting for something to turn
up might start with his own shirtsleeves.

No matter how well you nurse a
grudge, it will never get better.

A good deal of trouble has been caused
in the world by too much intelligence
and too little wisdom.

Afterword

When Marianne Bunge passed in December 2024, her family was unaware she had drafted three books of inspirational sayings during her life. The books were found as Marianne's office was being cleaned by her children. After reading the books, a publication posthumously was facilitated by the family with the hope that others would enjoy the same inspiration that Marianne passed along to her family and friends.

ABOUT THE AUTHOR

Marianne Bunge, 1937–2024, grew up in a small town in northern Wisconsin. She graduated high school with honors in the 1950s, married her high school sweetheart, and began raising her family of five children. She volunteered at church, led a 4-H group, opened up her home to foster children, and worked as a legal secretary until she retired.

Many friends sought Marianne's advice. She was at her best when she could be of help to others. Every day, Marianne spoke with friends and family. She was bright and cheery, offering her ear, her friendship, and her advice to all. She passed unexpectedly but quietly in December 2024.

About the Photographer:

Jennifer Beach has been taking pictures since before there were digital cameras. She has had a few of her photographs published in a national magazine alongside articles she authored. Her mother encouraged Jennifer to go professional. Jennifer says she enjoys a steady income too much.

www.ingramcontent.com/pod-product-compliance
Lightning Source LLC
Chambersburg PA
CBHW042027050526
44107CB00103B/720